Casseroles and One-Dish Meals

Contents

Shrimp & Corn Chowder
with Sun-Dried Tomatoes
Recipe on page 34

Fuss-free preparation and easy clean-up means...

Complete Satisfaction

Wouldn't you love to never have to compromise when making dinner? For convenience sake, we might be tempted to skimp on side dishes or sacrifice variety for simplicity. But one-dish meals are a win-win solution.

One-dish recipes streamline menu planning and food preparation, and they cut down on clean-up. Yet they still satisfy everyone's basic craving for hot, hearty, home cooked meals. Layers of flavors and a well-rounded profile that usually includes protein, vegetable, and starch all add up to total satisfaction for everyone.

This Campbell's® collection of one-dish recipes features favorite casseroles that go fresh from the oven to the table with minimal fuss, skillet suppers that whip together quickly on the stovetop, plus yummy soups, stews, and chilis that only require a basket of bread or rolls to turn into dinner. You'll also discover ethnically inspired dishes from around the world and easy updates on the classics sure to win everyone over, including the cook!

Home-baked and hearty casseroles

Favorites
From the Oven

Roast Pork with Green Apples & Golden Squash

Prep Time: 20 minutes
Bake Time: 45 minutes
Stand Time: 10 minutes

Vegetable cooking spray

2 (¾ pound **each**) whole pork tenderloins

1 teaspoon olive oil

¼ teaspoon coarsely ground black pepper

3 large Granny Smith apples, cored and thickly sliced

1½ pounds butternut squash, peeled and cubed (about 4 cups)

2 tablespoons packed brown sugar

½ teaspoon ground cinnamon

1 can (14 ounces) Swanson® Chicken **or** Natural Goodness™ Chicken Broth (1¾ cups)

2 teaspoons all-purpose flour

PREHEAT oven to 425°F. Spray large roasting pan with cooking spray.

BRUSH pork with oil and sprinkle with black pepper. Place in prepared pan. Mix apples, squash, brown sugar, cinnamon and ½ **cup** broth. Add to pan.

ROAST for 25 minutes or until temperature reads 155°F. on meat thermometer, stirring squash mixture once during roasting. Remove pork from pan and let stand 10 minutes. Roast squash mixture 15 minutes or until browned. Remove squash mixture from pan.

MIX remaining broth and flour. Stir into pan drippings, scraping up browned bits. Cook until mixture boils and thickens, stirring constantly. Serve sauce with sliced pork and squash mixture.

Serves 8.

Baked Pork Chops with Apple Raisin Stuffing

Prep Time: 15 minutes
Bake Time: 35 minutes

1   cup applesauce

½   cup water

2   tablespoons margarine **or** butter, melted

1   stalk celery, chopped (about ½ cup)

2   tablespoons raisins

4   cups Pepperidge Farm® Herb Seasoned Stuffing

4   boneless pork chops, ¾-inch thick (about 1 pound)

    Paprika **or** ground cinnamon

    Apple slices (optional)

MIX applesauce, water, margarine, celery and raisins. Add stuffing. Mix lightly. Spoon into 2-quart shallow baking dish. Arrange chops over stuffing. Sprinkle paprika over chops.

BAKE at 400°F. for 35 minutes or until chops are no longer pink. Top with apple slices, if desired.

Serves 4.

Beef Taco Bake

Prep Time: 10 minutes
Bake Time: 30 minutes

1   pound ground beef

1   can (10¾ ounces) Campbell's® Condensed Tomato Soup

1   cup Pace® Chunky Salsa **or** Picante Sauce

½   cup milk

6   (8-inch) flour tortillas **or** 8 (6-inch) corn tortillas, cut into 1-inch pieces

1   cup shredded Cheddar cheese (4 ounces)

COOK beef in medium skillet over medium-high heat until beef is browned, stirring to separate meat. Pour off fat.

ADD soup, salsa, milk, tortillas and **half** the cheese. Spoon into 2-quart shallow baking dish. **Cover**.

BAKE at 400°F. for 30 minutes or until hot. Sprinkle with remaining cheese.

Serves 4.

Beef Taco Bake

Tomato-Topped Chicken & Stuffing

Prep Time: 10 minutes
Bake Time: 30 minutes

- 5 cups Pepperidge Farm® Cubed Herb Seasoned Stuffing
- 6 tablespoons butter **or** margarine, melted
- $1\frac{1}{4}$ cups boiling water
- 4 to 6 skinless, boneless chicken breast halves (about 1 to $1\frac{1}{2}$ pounds)
- 1 can ($10\frac{3}{4}$ ounces) Campbell's® Condensed Cream of Chicken **or** 98% Fat Free Cream of Chicken Soup
- $\frac{1}{3}$ cup milk
- 1 medium tomato, sliced

CRUSH 1 cup stuffing. Mix with **2 tablespoons** butter for topping.

MIX remaining stuffing, remaining butter and water. Mix lightly. Spoon stuffing into 3-quart shallow baking dish. Top with chicken.

MIX soup and milk. Pour over chicken. Top with tomato and sprinkle with topping.

BAKE at 400°F. for 30 minutes or until chicken is no longer pink.

Serves 4 to 6.

Cornbread Chicken Pot Pie

Prep Time: 5 minutes
Bake Time: 30 minutes

- 1 can ($10\frac{3}{4}$ ounces) Campbell's® Condensed Cream of Chicken **or** 98% Fat Free Cream of Chicken Soup
- 1 can (about 8 ounces) whole kernel corn, drained
- 2 cups cubed cooked chicken **or** turkey
- 1 package ($8\frac{1}{2}$ ounces) corn muffin mix
- $\frac{3}{4}$ cup milk
- 1 egg
- $\frac{1}{2}$ cup shredded Cheddar cheese (2 ounces)

PREHEAT oven to 400°F. Mix soup, corn and chicken in 9-inch pie plate.

MIX muffin mix, milk and egg. Pour over chicken mixture.

BAKE for 30 minutes or until golden. Sprinkle with cheese.

Serves 4.

Cornbread Chicken Pot Pie

Garlic Mashed Potatoes & Beef Bake

Prep/Bake Time: 30 minutes

1   pound ground beef **or** ground turkey

1   can (10¾ ounces) Campbell's® Condensed Cream of Mushroom with Roasted Garlic Soup

1   tablespoon Worcestershire sauce

1   bag (16 ounces) frozen vegetable combination (broccoli, cauliflower, carrots), thawed

2   cups water

3   tablespoons margarine **or** butter

¾   cup milk

2   cups instant mashed potatoes

COOK beef in skillet until browned. Pour off fat.

MIX beef, ½ **can** soup, Worcestershire and vegetables in 2-quart shallow baking dish.

MIX water, margarine and remaining soup in saucepan. Heat to a boil. Remove from heat. Stir in milk. Slowly stir in potatoes. Spoon potatoes over beef mixture.

BAKE at 400°F. for 20 minutes or until hot.

Serves 4.

TIP:
Serve with a mixed green salad topped with orange sections, walnut pieces and raspberry vinaigrette. For dessert serve your favorite fruit dish.

3-Cheese Pasta Bake

Prep/Bake Time: 25 minutes

1   can (10¾ ounces)
    Campbell's® Condensed
    Cream of Mushroom **or**
    98% Fat Free Cream of
    Mushroom Soup

1   package (8 ounces)
    shredded two-cheese
    blend

⅓   cup grated Parmesan
    cheese

1   cup milk

¼   teaspoon ground black
    pepper

4   cups cooked corkscrew
    pasta

MIX soup, cheeses, milk and
black pepper in 1½-quart
casserole. Stir in pasta.

BAKE at 400°F. for 20 minutes
or until hot.

Serves 4.

TIP:
Use **2 cups** of your favorite
shredded cheese for the 8-ounce
package.

Shrimp Stuffing Au Gratin

Prep Time: 15 minutes
Bake Time: 30 minutes

$4\frac{1}{2}$ cups Pepperidge Farm® Herb Seasoned Stuffing

3 tablespoons butter **or** margarine, melted

$1\frac{1}{4}$ cups water

2 cups cooked broccoli flowerets

2 cups cooked medium shrimp

1 can ($10\frac{3}{4}$ ounces) Campbell's® Condensed Cream of Mushroom **or** 98% Fat Free Cream of Mushroom Soup

$\frac{1}{2}$ cup milk

2 tablespoons diced pimiento (optional)

1 cup shredded Swiss cheese (4 ounces)

CRUSH $\frac{1}{2}$ **cup** stuffing and mix with **1 tablespoon** butter.

MIX water and remaining butter. Add remaining stuffing. Mix lightly. Spoon into 2-quart shallow baking dish.

TOP with broccoli and shrimp. Mix soup, milk, pimiento and cheese. Pour over shrimp mixture. Sprinkle with stuffing mixture.

BAKE at 350°F. for 30 minutes or until hot.

Serves 6.

TIP

For **2 cups** cooked medium shrimp, cook **1 pound** medium shrimp in medium saucepan over medium heat in **4 cups** boiling water for 1 to 3 minutes or until shrimp turn pink. Rinse immediately under cold water. Shell and devein.

TIP:

For **2 cups** cooked broccoli flowerets use **3 cups** fresh broccoli flowerets.

TIP:

To melt margarine, remove wrapper and place in microwavable cup. Cover and microwave on **HIGH** 45 seconds.

Lemon-Basil Turkey with Roasted Vegetables

Prep Time: 20 minutes
Bake Time: 1 hour 30 minutes

Vegetable cooking spray

2 medium lemons

8 pound turkey breast

1 tablespoon butter **or** margarine, melted

24 baby Yukon gold potatoes

1 pound butternut squash, peeled and cut into 1-inch cubes (about 3 cups)

8 medium beets, peeled and cut into 1-inch cubes ($3\frac{3}{4}$ cups)

Lemon-Basil Turkey with Roasted Vegetables

12 small white boiling onions **or** 1 cup frozen whole onions

1 tablespoon dried basil leaves, crushed

1 cup Swanson® Chicken **or** Natural Goodness™ Chicken Broth

SPRAY 17×11-inch roasting pan with cooking spray.

CUT 1 lemon into thin slices. Juice remaining lemon and reserve **2 tablespoons** juice.

Loosen skin on turkey breast and place lemon slices under skin. Brush turkey with butter. Place turkey and vegetables in prepared pan. Sprinkle with basil. Mix broth and lemon juice. Pour **half** of broth mixture over turkey.

ROAST at 375°F. for 1 hour.

STIR vegetables. Add remaining broth mixture to pan. Roast 30 minutes or until turkey is no longer pink and vegetables are tender.

Serves 8.

Thyme Chicken & Roasted Winter Vegetables

Prep Time: 15 minutes
Bake Time: 1 hour 30 minutes

Vegetable cooking spray

3   pound broiler-fryer chicken, cut up

1   tablespoon butter **or** margarine, melted

4   medium red potatoes (about $1\frac{1}{4}$ pounds), cut into quarters

4   medium carrots (about $\frac{3}{4}$ pound), peeled and cut into 2-inch pieces

6   medium parsnips (about 1 pound), peeled and cut into 2-inch pieces

1   cup Brussels sprouts, cut in half

4   medium onions, cut into quarters

1   tablespoon chopped fresh thyme leaves **or** 1 teaspoon dried thyme leaves, crushed

1   cup Swanson® Chicken **or** Natural Goodness™ Chicken Broth

$\frac{1}{2}$ cup Chablis **or** other dry white wine

SPRAY large roasting pan with cooking spray. Place chicken in prepared pan. Brush with butter.

PLACE potatoes, carrots, parsnips, Brussels sprouts and onions around chicken. Sprinkle with thyme. Mix broth and wine and pour **half** of broth mixture over chicken and vegetables.

ROAST at 375°F. for 1 hour or until chicken is no longer pink. Remove chicken from pan and keep warm.

STIR vegetables. Add remaining broth mixture to pan. Roast for 30 minutes or until vegetables are tender.

Serves 4.

Fiesta Chicken Casserole

Prep Time: 15 minutes
Bake Time: 40 minutes

1 package (15 ounces)
   refrigerated pie crusts

1 jar (16 ounces) Pace®
   Chunky Salsa

1 can (10¾ ounces)
   Campbell's® Condensed
   Cream of Chicken **or**
   98% Fat Free Cream of
   Chicken Soup

1 cup sour cream

2 cups shredded Cheddar
   cheese (8 ounces)

1 package (24 ounces)
   frozen whole kernel corn

2 cans (9.75 ounces each)
   Swanson® Premium
   Chunk Chicken Breast,
   drained

1 can (about 15 ounces)
   black beans, drained and
   rinsed

PREHEAT oven to 400°F. Bring
pie crust to room temperature.

MIX salsa, soup, sour cream,
cheese, corn, chicken and beans in
large bowl. Spoon into ungreased
13×9×2-inch baking pan.

PLACE crusts on floured surface,
overlapping about 3 inches in the
center. Press seam to seal. Roll
into 14- by 10-inch rectangle.
Trim excess crust. Place crust over
beef mixture and flute edges. Cut
slits in pastry.

BAKE for 40 to 45 minutes or
until pie crust is golden brown.

Serves 6.

Baked Chicken & Cheese Risotto

Prep Time: 10 minutes
Bake Time: 45 minutes
Stand Time: 5 minutes

1   can (10¾ ounces)
        Campbell's® Condensed
        Cream of Mushroom **or**
        98% Fat Free Cream of
        Mushroom Soup

1¼ cups water

½   cup milk

¼   cup shredded part-skim
        mozzarella cheese
        (1 ounce)

3   tablespoons grated
        Parmesan cheese

1½ cups frozen mixed
        vegetables

½   pound skinless, boneless
        chicken breasts, cut into
        cubes

¾   cup **uncooked** Arborio **or**
        regular long-grain white
        rice

MIX soup, water, milk, mozzarella cheese, Parmesan cheese, vegetables, chicken and rice in 3-quart shallow baking dish. **Cover**.

BAKE at 400°F. for 35 minutes. Stir.

BAKE for 10 minutes or until hot and rice is done. Let stand 5 minutes.

Serves 4.

Country Chicken Casserole

Prep Time: 10 minutes
Bake Time: 25 minutes

1 can (10¾ ounces) Campbell's® Condensed Cream of Celery **or** 98% Fat Free Cream of Celery Soup

1 can (10¾ ounces) Campbell's® Condensed Cream of Potato Soup

1 cup milk

¼ teaspoon dried thyme leaves, crushed

⅛ teaspoon ground black pepper

4 cups cooked cut-up vegetables

2 cups cubed cooked chicken **or** turkey

1½ cups water

4 tablespoons margarine **or** butter

4 cups Pepperidge Farm® Herb Seasoned Stuffing

MIX soups, milk, thyme, black pepper, vegetables and chicken in 3-quart shallow baking dish.

HEAT water and margarine to a boil in medium saucepan over high heat. Add stuffing. Mix lightly. Spoon stuffing over chicken mixture.

BAKE at 400°F. for 25 minutes or until hot.

Serves 5.

Chicken Asparagus Gratin

Prep Time: 20 minutes
Bake Time: 30 minutes

1 can (10¾ ounces) Campbell's® Condensed Cream of Asparagus Soup

½ cup milk

¼ teaspoon onion powder

⅛ teaspoon ground black pepper

3 cups hot cooked corkscrew pasta

1½ cups cubed cooked chicken

1½ cups cooked cut asparagus

1 cup shredded Cheddar **or** Swiss cheese (4 ounces)

MIX soup, milk, onion powder and black pepper in 2-quart shallow baking dish. Stir in pasta, chicken, asparagus and ½ **cup** cheese.

BAKE at 400°F. for 25 minutes or until hot. Stir.

SPRINKLE with remaining cheese. Bake 5 minutes or until cheese is melted.

Serves 4.

Chicken Asparagus Gratin

Chicken and Peppers Pie

Prep Time: 10 minutes
Bake Time: 30 minutes

1   can (10¾ ounces) Campbell's® Condensed Cream of Chicken **or** 98% Fat Free Cream of Chicken Soup

½   cup Pace® Picante Sauce

½   cup sour cream

2   teaspoons chili powder

1   jar (7 ounces) whole roasted sweet peppers, drained and cut into strips

4   green onions, sliced (about ½ cup)

3   cups cubed cooked chicken

1   package (11 ounces) refrigerated cornbread twists

Fresh sage leaves (optional)

MIX soup, picante sauce, sour cream, chili powder, peppers, green onions and chicken in 2-quart shallow baking dish.

BAKE at 400°F. for 15 minutes. Stir.

SEPARATE bread twists into **16** strips. Arrange strips, lattice-fashion, over chicken mixture, overlapping strips as necessary to fit.

BAKE for 15 minutes or until bread is golden. Top with sage, if desired.

Serves 6.

Turkey Stuffing Divan

Prep Time: 10 minutes
Bake Time: 30 minutes

1¼   cups boiling water

4   tablespoons butter **or** margarine, melted

4   cups Pepperidge Farm® Herb Seasoned Stuffing

2   cups cooked broccoli cuts

2   cups cubed cooked turkey **or** chicken

1   can (10¾ ounces) Campbell's® Condensed Cream of Celery **or** 98% Fat Free Cream of Celery Soup

½   cup milk

1   cup shredded Cheddar cheese (4 ounces)

MIX water and butter. Add stuffing. Mix lightly.

SPOON into 2-quart shallow baking dish. Top with broccoli and turkey.

MIX soup, milk and ½ **cup** cheese and pour over turkey mixture. Sprinkle with remaining cheese.

BAKE at 350°F. for 30 minutes or until hot.

Serves 6.

Turkey Stuffing Divan

Chicken Florentine Lasagna

Prep Time: 10 minutes
Bake Time: 1 hour
Stand Time: 5 minutes

2 cans (10¾ ounces **each**)
   Campbell's® Condensed
   Cream of Chicken with
   Herbs Soup

2 cups milk

1 egg

1 container (15 ounces)
   ricotta cheese

6 **uncooked** lasagna
   noodles

1 package (about
   10 ounces) frozen
   chopped spinach,
   thawed and well drained

2 cups cubed cooked
   chicken **or** turkey

2 cups shredded Cheddar
   cheese (8 ounces)

MIX soup and milk.

MIX egg and ricotta cheese.

SPREAD **1 cup** soup mixture in 3-quart shallow baking dish. Top with **3 uncooked** lasagna noodles, ricotta mixture, spinach, chicken, **1 cup** Cheddar cheese and **1 cup** soup mixture. Top with remaining **3 uncooked** lasagna noodles and remaining soup mixture. **Cover.**

BAKE at 375°F. for 1 hour. Uncover and top with remaining Cheddar cheese. Let stand 5 minutes.

Serves 6.

TIP:
To thaw spinach, microwave on **HIGH** 3 minutes, breaking apart with a fork halfway through heating.

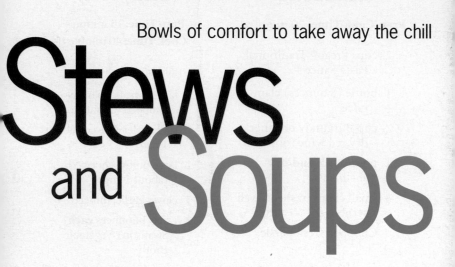

Bowls of comfort to take away the chill

Stews and Soups

Slow Cooker Hearty Beef & Bean Chili

Prep Time: 15 minutes
Cook Time: 8 to 10 hours

1½ pounds ground beef

1 can (10¾ ounces) Campbell's® Condensed Tomato Soup

½ cup water

¼ cup chili powder

2 teaspoons ground cumin

2 cloves garlic, minced

1 large onion, chopped (about 1 cup)

2 cans (about 15 ounces **each**) red kidney beans, drained

1 can (14½ ounces) diced tomatoes

COOK beef in medium skillet over medium-high heat until beef is browned, stirring to separate meat. Pour off fat.

MIX beef, soup, water, chili powder, cumin, garlic, onion, beans and tomatoes in 3½-quart slow cooker.

COVER and cook on LOW 8 to 10 hours*.

Serves 6.

*Or on HIGH 4 to 5 hours

20-Minute Seafood Stew

Prep/Cook Time: 20 minutes

- 2 cups Prego® Traditional Pasta Sauce
- 1 bottle (8 ounces) clam juice
- ¼ cup Burgundy **or** other dry red wine (optional)
- 1 pound fish **and/or** shellfish*
- 8 small clams in shells, well scrubbed
  Chopped fresh parsley

MIX pasta sauce, clam juice and wine in large saucepan. Heat to a boil. Cook over low heat 5 minutes.

ADD fish and clams. Cover and cook 5 minutes or until fish flakes easily when tested with fork and clams are open. Discard any clams that do not open. Sprinkle with parsley.

Serves 4.

*Use any one **or** a combination of the following: Firm white fish fillets (cut into 2-inch pieces), boneless fish steaks (cut into 1-inch cubes), medium shrimp (shelled and deveined) **or** scallops.*

TIP:
Before cooking, discard any clams that remain open when tapped.

Hearty Bean & Barley Soup

Prep Time: 15 minutes
Cook Time: 40 minutes

- 1 tablespoon olive oil
- 2 large carrots, coarsely chopped (about 1 cup)
- 2 stalks celery, sliced (about 1 cup)
- 1 large onion, chopped (about 1 cup)
- 3 cloves garlic, minced
- 2 cans (14 ounces **each**) Swanson® Vegetable Broth
- 1 can (about 15 ounces) red kidney beans, rinsed and drained
- 1 can (14½ ounces) diced tomatoes
- ¼ cup **uncooked** pearl barley
- 2 cups firmly packed chopped fresh spinach leaves
  Ground black pepper

HEAT oil in saucepot over medium heat. Add carrots, celery, onion and garlic and cook until tender.

ADD broth, beans, tomatoes and barley. Heat to a boil. Cover and cook over low heat 30 minutes or until barley is done.

STIR in spinach and season to taste with black pepper. Heat through.

Serves 6.

Spaghetti Soup

Prep Time: 15 minutes
Cook Time: 30 minutes

2 tablespoons vegetable oil

$\frac{1}{2}$ pound skinless, boneless chicken breasts, cut into cubes

1 medium onion, chopped (about $\frac{1}{2}$ cup)

1 large carrot, chopped (about $\frac{1}{2}$ cup)

1 stalk celery, finely chopped (about $\frac{1}{3}$ cup)

2 cloves garlic, minced

4 cups Swanson® Chicken **or** Natural Goodness™ Chicken Broth

1 can ($10\frac{3}{4}$ ounces) Campbell's® Condensed Tomato Soup

1 cup water

3 ounces spaghetti, broken into 1-inch pieces

2 tablespoons chopped fresh parsley (optional)

HEAT 1 tablespoon oil in saucepot over medium-high heat. Add chicken and cook until browned, stirring often. Remove chicken.

ADD remaining oil and heat over medium heat. Add onion and cook 1 minute. Add carrots. Cook 1 minute. Add celery and garlic. Cook 1 minute.

ADD broth, soup and water. Heat to a boil.

ADD pasta. Cook about 10 minutes or until pasta is tender. Add chicken and parsley, if desired and heat through.

Serves 4.

Picante Pork Stew

Prep Time: 20 minutes
Cook Time: 25 minutes

1   pound boneless pork loin

3   tablespoons cornstarch

1   can (14 ounces) Swanson®
    Vegetable Broth

2   tablespoons vegetable oil

4   cups cut-up fresh
    vegetables*

½   cup Pace® Picante Sauce

SLICE pork into very thin strips.
Mix cornstarch and broth until
smooth. Set aside.

HEAT 1 tablespoon oil in saucepot
over medium-high heat. Add pork
and cook until browned, stirring
often. Set pork aside.

ADD remaining oil and heat over
medium heat. Add vegetables and
cook until tender-crisp. Pour off
fat.

ADD picante sauce. Stir cornstarch
mixture and add. Cook until
mixture boils and thickens, stirring
constantly. Return pork to pan and
heat through.

Serves 4.

*Use asparagus cut into 2-inch
pieces, red pepper cut into 2-inch-
long strips and sliced onions*

TIP:
To make slicing easier, freeze pork
1 hour.

Shrimp & Corn Chowder with Sun-Dried Tomatoes

Prep/Cook Time: 20 minutes

1   can (10¾ ounces)
      Campbell's® Condensed
      Cream of Potato Soup

1½   cups half-and-half

2   cups whole kernel corn

2   tablespoons sun-dried
      tomatoes cut in strips

1   cup small **or** medium
      cooked shrimp

2   tablespoons chopped fresh
      chives

      Ground black **or** ground
      red pepper

MIX soup, half-and-half, corn and
tomatoes in medium saucepan over
medium heat. Heat to a boil. Cover
and cook over low heat 10 minutes.

STIR in shrimp and chives and
heat through. Season to taste with
black pepper.

Serves 4.

TIP:
For a lighter version, substitute
skim milk for the half-and-half.

**Shrimp & Corn Chowder with
Sun-Dried Tomatoes**

Spicy Mexican Minestrone Stew

Prep Time: 15 minutes
Cook Time: 35 minutes

$\frac{1}{2}$ pound sweet Italian pork sausage, casing removed

2 teaspoons vegetable oil

1 can (14 ounces) Swanson® Beef **or** Lower Sodium Beef Broth (1$\frac{3}{4}$ cups)

1$\frac{1}{2}$ cups Pace® Picante Sauce

$\frac{1}{4}$ teaspoon garlic powder **or** 2 cloves garlic, minced

1 can (14$\frac{1}{2}$ ounces) whole peeled tomatoes, cut up

1 cup **uncooked** medium shell pasta

1 package (about 10 ounces) frozen cut green beans, thawed (about 2 cups)

1 can (about 15 ounces) kidney beans, drained

SHAPE sausage **firmly** into $\frac{1}{2}$-inch meatballs.

HEAT oil in saucepot over medium-high heat. Add meatballs and cook until evenly browned. Set meatballs aside. Pour off fat.

ADD broth, picante sauce, garlic and tomatoes. Heat to a boil. Stir in pasta. Return meatballs to pan. Cover and cook over low heat 10 minutes, stirring often.

ADD green beans and kidney beans and cook 10 minutes or until pasta is done, stirring occasionally.

Serves 6.

TIP:
Substitute **1 can** (about 16 ounces) cut green beans, drained for frozen beans.

TIP:
For quicker preparation, cook Italian sausage in oil until meat is browned, stirring to separate meat. Pour off fat.

Italian Sausage & Lentil Stew

Prep Time: 15 minutes
Cook Time: 55 minutes

Vegetable cooking spray

1 pound sweet Italian pork sausage, cut into 1-inch pieces

2 large carrots, sliced (about 1 cup)

1 large onion, chopped (about 1 cup)

2 cloves garlic, minced

2 cans (14 ounces **each**) Swanson® Vegetable Broth

2 teaspoons dried oregano leaves, crushed **or** 2 tablespoons chopped fresh oregano

Italian Sausage & Lentil Stew

1 bay leaf

2 cups cubed red-skinned potatoes

½ cup dried lentils

2 cups coarsely chopped broccoli rabe

SPRAY saucepot with cooking spray and heat over medium-high heat 1 minute. Add sausage and cook until browned, stirring often. Pour off fat.

ADD carrots, onion and garlic and cook until tender.

ADD broth, oregano, bay leaf, potatoes and lentils. Heat to a boil. Cover and cook over low heat 40 minutes or until lentils are done.

STIR in broccoli rabe and cook 5 minutes. Remove bay leaf.

Serves 8.

Herb-Simmered Beef Stew

Prep Time: 15 minutes
Cook Time: 1 hour 30 minutes

- 2 pounds beef for stew, cut into 1-inch pieces

  Ground black pepper

- 2 tablespoons all-purpose flour

- 2 tablespoons olive oil

- 3 cups thickly sliced mushrooms (about 8 ounces)

- 3 cloves garlic, minced

- ½ teaspoon **each** dried marjoram, thyme **and** rosemary leaves, crushed **or** 1½ teaspoons **each** chopped fresh marjoram, thyme **and** rosemary

- 1 bay leaf

- 1 can (14 ounces) Swanson® Beef **or** Lower Sodium Beef Broth (1¾ cups)

- 3 cups fresh **or** frozen baby carrots

- 12 whole baby red-skinned potatoes, with a strip of peel removed in center

SPRINKLE beef with black pepper and coat with flour.

HEAT oil in saucepot over medium-high heat. Add beef and cook until browned, stirring often.

ADD mushrooms, garlic, herbs and bay leaf and cook until mushrooms are tender and liquid is evaporated.

ADD broth. Heat to a boil. Cover and cook over low heat 45 minutes.

ADD carrots and potatoes. Heat to a boil. Cover and cook over low heat 30 minutes or until beef is fork-tender. Remove bay leaf.

Serves 6.

Country Chicken Stew

Prep Time: 15 minutes
Cook Time: 40 minutes

2   slices bacon, diced

1   medium onion, sliced
    (about $\frac{1}{2}$ cup)

1   can (10$\frac{3}{4}$ ounces)
    Campbell's® Condensed
    Cream of Chicken **or**
    98% Fat Free Cream of
    Chicken Soup

1   soup can water

$\frac{1}{2}$ teaspoon dried oregano
    leaves, crushed

3   medium potatoes (about
    1 pound), cut into
    1-inch pieces

2   medium carrots, sliced
    (about 1 cup)

1   cup frozen cut green
    beans

2   cans (4.5 ounces **each**)
    Swanson® Premium
    Chunk Chicken Breast,
    drained

2   tablespoons chopped
    fresh parsley

COOK bacon in medium skillet
over medium heat until crisp.
Remove and drain on paper
towels.

ADD onion and cook in hot
drippings until tender.

ADD soup, water, oregano,
potatoes and carrots. Heat to a
boil. Cover and cook over low
heat 15 minutes.

ADD beans. Cover and cook
10 minutes or until vegetables
are tender. Add bacon, chicken
and parsley and heat through.

Serves 4.

TIP:
Substitute **1 can** (8 ounces) cut
green beans, drained for frozen
beans. Add to skillet with
chicken.

Smokin' Texas Chili

Prep Time: 15 minutes
Cook Time: 1 hour 45 minutes

2   tablespoons olive oil

1$\frac{1}{2}$ pounds boneless beef
    sirloin **or** top round
    steak, $\frac{3}{4}$-inch thick, cut
    into $\frac{1}{2}$-inch pieces

1   medium onion, chopped
    (about $\frac{1}{2}$ cup)

2   cloves garlic, minced

3   cups Pace® Chunky Salsa,
    any variety

$\frac{1}{2}$ cup water

1   tablespoon chili powder

1   teaspoon ground cumin

1   can (about 15 ounces)
    red kidney beans,
    rinsed and drained

$\frac{1}{4}$ cup chopped fresh
    cilantro leaves

    Chili Toppings*

Smokin' Texas Chili

HEAT 1 tablespoon oil in saucepot over medium-high heat. Add beef in 2 batches and cook until browned, stirring often. Remove beef.

ADD remaining oil and heat over medium heat. Add onion and cook until tender. Add garlic and cook 30 seconds.

ADD salsa, water, chili powder and cumin. Heat to a boil.

Return beef to saucepot. Add beans. Cover and cook over low heat 1 hour. Uncover and cook 30 minutes or until beef is fork-tender.

SPRINKLE with cilantro and toppings, if desired.

Serves 6.

Chopped tomatoes, chopped onions **or shredded cheese*

Whip up a meal with just one pan to wash

Supper in a Skillet

New Orleans Shrimp Toss

New Orleans Shrimp Toss

Prep/Cook Time: 20 minutes

1 pound fresh large shrimp, shelled and deveined

2 tablespoons vegetable oil

2 tablespoons lemon juice

1 tablespoon Worcestershire sauce

1 teaspoon Cajun seasoning

1 medium onion, chopped (about $\frac{1}{2}$ cup)

2 cloves garlic, minced

1 can ($10\frac{3}{4}$ ounces) Campbell's® Condensed Cream of Chicken with Herbs Soup

$\frac{1}{2}$ cup milk

1 teaspoon paprika

Cornbread **or** biscuits

2 tablespoons chopped fresh chives

MIX shrimp, **1 tablespoon** oil, lemon juice, Worcestershire and Cajun seasoning.

HEAT remaining oil in medium skillet over medium heat. Add onion and garlic and cook until tender.

ADD soup, milk and paprika. Heat to a boil. Add shrimp mixture. Cover and cook over low heat 5 minutes or until shrimp turn pink. Serve with cornbread. Sprinkle with chives.

Serves 4.

Beefy Vegetable Skillet

Prep/Cook Time: 20 minutes
Stand Time: 5 minutes

1 pound ground beef

1 medium onion, chopped (about $\frac{1}{2}$ cup)

2 medium zucchini, cut into quarters lengthwise and sliced (about 2 cups)

1 can (about $14\frac{1}{2}$ ounces) stewed tomatoes

2 cups Pepperidge Farm® Cubed Herb Seasoned Stuffing

2 tablespoons grated Parmesan cheese

COOK beef and onion in medium skillet over medium-high heat until beef is browned, stirring to separate meat. Pour off fat.

ADD zucchini and tomatoes. Heat to a boil. Cover and cook over low heat 5 minutes or until zucchini is tender. Remove from heat.

ADD stuffing and cheese. Mix lightly. Cover and let stand 5 minutes. Serve with additional cheese if desired.

Serves 4.

Southwest Skillet

Prep/Cook Time: 25 minutes
Stand Time: 5 minutes

- $\frac{3}{4}$ pound ground beef
- 1 tablespoon chili powder
- 1 can (10$\frac{3}{4}$ ounces) Campbell's® Condensed Beefy Mushroom Soup
- $\frac{1}{4}$ cup water
- 1 can (14$\frac{1}{2}$ ounces) whole peeled tomatoes, cut up
- 1 can (about 15 ounces) kidney beans, rinsed and drained
- $\frac{3}{4}$ cup **uncooked** instant white rice
- $\frac{1}{2}$ cup shredded Cheddar cheese (2 ounces)

  Tortilla chips

COOK beef with chili powder in medium skillet over medium-high heat until beef is browned, stirring to separate meat. Pour off fat.

ADD soup, water, tomatoes and beans. Heat to a boil. Cover and cook over low heat 10 minutes. Remove from heat.

STIR in rice. Cover and let stand 5 minutes. Top with cheese. Serve with tortilla chips.

Serves 4.

Chicken & Stuffing Skillet

Prep/Cook Time: 20 minutes

- 1 tablespoon butter **or** margarine
- 4 skinless, boneless chicken breast halves (about 1 pound)
- 1 box (6 ounces) chicken flavor stuffing mix
- 1 can (10$\frac{3}{4}$ ounces) Campbell's® Condensed Cream of Mushroom **or** 98% Fat Free Cream of Mushroom Soup
- $\frac{1}{2}$ cup milk
- $\frac{1}{2}$ cup shredded Cheddar cheese (2 ounces)

HEAT butter in medium skillet over medium-high heat. Add chicken and cook 12 to 15 minutes or until chicken is no longer pink. Remove chicken.

PREPARE stuffing in skillet according to package directions **except** let stand 2 minutes.

RETURN chicken to skillet. Mix soup and milk. Pour over chicken. Sprinkle with cheese. Cover and heat through.

Serves 4.

Chicken & Stuffing Skillet

Zesty Turkey & Rice

Prep Time: 5 minutes
Cook Time: 30 minutes

1 can (14 ounces) Swanson® Chicken **or** Natural Goodness™ Chicken Broth (1¼ cups)

1 teaspoon dried basil leaves, crushed

¼ teaspoon garlic powder

¼ teaspoon hot pepper sauce

1 can (about 14½ ounces) stewed tomatoes

¾ cup **uncooked** regular long-grain white rice

1 cup frozen peas

2 cups cubed cooked turkey **or** chicken

MIX broth, basil, garlic powder, hot pepper sauce and tomatoes in medium saucepan over medium-high heat. Heat to a boil. Stir in rice. Cover and cook over low heat 20 minutes.

STIR in peas and turkey. Cover and cook 5 minutes or until rice is done.

Serves 4.

Sausage and Broccoli Skillet

Prep/Cook Time: 25 minutes

1½ pounds sweet Italian pork sausage, casing removed

1 medium onion, chopped (about ½ cup)

2 cloves garlic, minced

1 can (10¾ ounces) Campbell's® Condensed Cream of Broccoli **or** 98% Fat Free Cream of Broccoli Soup

½ cup milk

1 bag (about 16 ounces) frozen broccoli cuts

½ cup shredded Parmesan cheese

6 cups hot cooked corkscrew pasta (about 5 cups **uncooked**)

Crushed red pepper (optional)

COOK sausage in medium skillet over medium-high heat until sausage is browned, stirring to separate meat.

ADD onion and garlic. Cook over medium heat until tender. Pour off fat.

ADD soup, milk, broccoli and **¼ cup** cheese. Heat to a boil. Cover and cook over low heat 5 minutes or until broccoli is tender, stirring occasionally.

TOSS with pasta. Sprinkle with remaining cheese. Serve with red pepper, if desired.

Serves 6.

Sausage and Broccoli Skillet

Pork Chop Skillet Dinner

Prep Time: 10 minutes
Cook Time: 40 minutes

1 tablespoon olive **or** vegetable oil

4 pork chops, $\frac{3}{4}$-inch thick (about $1\frac{1}{2}$ pounds)

1 medium onion, chopped (about $\frac{1}{2}$ cup)

1 cup **uncooked** regular long-grain white rice

1 can ($10\frac{1}{2}$ ounces) Campbell's® Condensed Chicken Broth

1 cup orange juice

3 tablespoons chopped fresh parsley

4 orange slices

HEAT oil in medium skillet over medium-high heat. Add chops and cook 10 minutes or until browned. Set chops aside.

ADD onion and rice and cook until rice is browned. Stir in broth, orange juice and **2 tablespoons** parsley. Heat to a boil. Return chops to skillet.

COVER and cook over low heat 20 minutes or until rice is done. Top with orange slices and sprinkle with remaining parsley.

Serves 4.

Pasta with the Works

Prep/Cook Time: 25 minutes

1 medium green pepper, cut into 2-inch-long strips (about $1\frac{1}{2}$ cups)

$\frac{1}{2}$ cup thinly sliced pepperoni

2 cups Prego® Pasta Sauce with Fresh Mushrooms **or** Traditional Pasta Sauce

$\frac{1}{3}$ cup pitted ripe olives, cut in half (optional)

4 cups hot cooked corkscrew pasta

1 cup shredded mozzarella cheese (4 ounces)

Grated Parmesan cheese

COOK pepper and pepperoni in medium skillet over medium heat until pepper is tender-crisp, stirring often.

ADD pasta sauce and olives. Heat to a boil. Cover and cook over low heat 10 minutes.

STIR in pasta and mozzarella cheese. Serve with Parmesan cheese.

Serves 4.

Pasta with the Works

Citrus Chicken and Rice

Prep Time: 5 minutes
Cook Time: 35 minutes

4 skinless, boneless chicken breast halves (about 1 pound)

1 can (14 ounces) Swanson® Chicken **or** Natural Goodness™ Chicken Broth (1¼ cups)

½ cup orange juice

1 medium onion, chopped (about ½ cup)

1 cup **uncooked** regular long-grain white rice

3 tablespoons chopped fresh parsley **or** 1 tablespoon dried parsley flakes

Orange slices

COOK chicken in nonstick medium skillet over medium-high heat 10 minutes or until browned. Set chicken aside.

ADD broth, orange juice, onion and rice. Heat to a boil. Cover and cook over low heat 10 minutes.

RETURN chicken to skillet. Cover and cook 10 minutes or until chicken is no longer pink and rice is done. Stir in parsley and top with orange slices.

Serves 4.

Beef Taco Skillet

Prep/Cook Time: 20 minutes

1 pound ground beef

1 can (10¾ ounces) Campbell's® Condensed Tomato Soup

1 cup Pace® Chunky Salsa **or** Picante Sauce

½ cup water

8 corn **or** flour tortillas (6-inch), cut into 1-inch pieces

1 cup shredded Cheddar cheese (4 ounces)

COOK beef in medium skillet over medium-high heat until beef is browned, stirring to separate meat. Pour off fat.

ADD soup, salsa, water, tortillas and **half** the cheese. Heat to a boil. Cover and cook over low heat 5 minutes or until hot.

TOP with remaining cheese.

Serves 4.

Beef Taco Skillet

Wild Mushroom Chicken Balsamico

Prep Time: 10 minutes
Cook Time: 30 minutes

3 teaspoons olive **or** vegetable oil

4 skinless, boneless chicken breast halves (about 1 pound)

12 ounces assorted wild mushrooms (portobello, shiitake, oyster and/or crimini), sliced (about 3 cups)

1 medium zucchini, sliced (about 1½ cups)

1 medium onion, cut into wedges

2 cloves garlic, minced

2 cups Prego® Marinara Pasta Sauce

¼ cup balsamic vinegar

Freshly ground black pepper

HEAT 1 teaspoon oil in large nonstick skillet over medium-high heat. Add chicken and cook 10 minutes or until browned. Remove chicken.

HEAT remaining oil over medium heat. Add mushrooms, zucchini and onion and cook until tender. Add garlic and cook 1 minute.

ADD pasta sauce and vinegar. Heat to a boil. Return chicken to skillet. Cover and cook over low heat 10 minutes or until chicken is no longer pink. Serve with black pepper.

Serves 4.

Chicken & Noodles

Prep/Cook Time: 20 minutes

1 tablespoon vegetable oil

1 pound skinless, boneless chicken breasts, cut into cubes

1 can (10¾ ounces) Campbell's® Condensed Cream of Chicken **or** 98% Fat Free Cream of Chicken Soup

½ cup milk

⅛ teaspoon ground black pepper

3 cups cooked medium egg noodles

⅓ cup grated Parmesan cheese

HEAT oil in medium skillet over medium-high heat. Add chicken and cook until browned, stirring often.

ADD soup, milk, black pepper, noodles and cheese. Heat through.

Serves 4.

Chicken & Noodles

Chicken with White Beans

Prep Time: 10 minutes
Cook Time: 45 minutes

1 tablespoon vegetable oil

4 chicken breast halves (about 2 pounds)

2 cups Prego® Traditional Pasta Sauce

$\frac{1}{4}$ teaspoon garlic powder **or** 2 cloves garlic, minced

1 large onion, chopped (about 1 cup)

2 cans (about 16 ounces **each**) white kidney (cannellini) beans, rinsed and drained

HEAT oil in medium skillet over medium-high heat. Add chicken and cook 10 minutes or until browned.

ADD pasta sauce, garlic powder, onion and beans. Heat to a boil. Cover and cook over low heat 30 minutes or until chicken is no longer pink.

Serves 4.

TIP:
If desired, remove skin from chicken before browning.

Cheesy Chicken and Rice

Prep/Cook Time: 20 minutes

1 tablespoon vegetable oil

4 skinless, boneless chicken breast halves (about 1 pound)

1 can (10$\frac{3}{4}$ ounces) Campbell's® Condensed Cream of Chicken **or** 98% Fat Free Cream of Chicken Soup

1$\frac{1}{2}$ cups water

$\frac{1}{4}$ teaspoon paprika

$\frac{1}{4}$ teaspoon ground black pepper

2 cups **uncooked** instant white rice*

2 cups fresh **or** frozen broccoli flowerets

$\frac{1}{2}$ cup shredded Cheddar cheese (2 ounces)

HEAT oil in medium skillet over medium-high heat. Add chicken and cook 10 minutes or until browned. Remove chicken.

ADD soup, water, paprika and black pepper. Heat to a boil.

STIR in rice and broccoli. Return chicken to skillet. Sprinkle chicken with additional paprika and black pepper. Top with cheese. Cover and cook over low heat 5 minutes or until chicken is no longer pink and rice is done.

Serves 4.

*For creamier dish, use **1$\frac{1}{2}$ cups** rice.*

Cheesy Chicken and Rice

Lemon Asparagus Chicken

Prep/Cook Time: 20 minutes

1 tablespoon vegetable oil

4 skinless, boneless chicken breast halves (about 1 pound)

1 can (10¾ ounces) Campbell's® Condensed Cream of Asparagus Soup

¼ cup milk

1 tablespoon lemon juice

⅛ teaspoon ground black pepper

HEAT oil in medium skillet over medium-high heat. Add chicken and cook 10 minutes or until browned.

ADD soup, milk, lemon juice and black pepper. Heat to a boil. Cover and cook over low heat 5 minutes or until chicken is no longer pink.

Serves 4.

Fast Fiesta Shepherd's Pie

Prep/Cook Time: 20 minutes

1 pound ground beef

1 can (10¾ ounces) Campbell's® Condensed Tomato Soup

¾ cup Pace® Picante Sauce

1 teaspoon ground cumin

1 cup frozen whole kernel corn

1 can (11 ounces) Campbell's® Condensed Fiesta Nacho Cheese Soup

1 cup milk

2 tablespoons butter **or** margarine

1⅓ cups instant mashed potato flakes **or** buds

Chopped fresh cilantro leaves **or** parsley (optional)

COOK beef in medium skillet over medium-high heat until beef is browned, stirring to separate meat. Pour off fat.

ADD tomato soup, picante sauce, cumin and corn. Heat through over low heat.

HEAT cheese soup, milk and butter to a boil in medium saucepan over medium-high heat. Remove from heat. Stir in potato flakes. Let stand 30 seconds. Mix with fork until evenly moistened. Drop potatoes by large spoonfuls onto beef mixture. Sprinkle with cilantro, if desired.

Serves 4.

Fast Fiesta Shepherd's Pie

Skillet Sausage and Stuffing

Prep Time: 10 minutes
Cook Time: 20 minutes
Stand Time: 5 minutes

- 1   pound sweet **or** hot Italian pork sausage, cut into 1-inch pieces
- 1¼   cups water*
- 1   medium onion, cut into wedges
- 1   small green **or** red pepper, cut into 2-inch-long strips (about 1 cup)
- 4   cups Pepperidge Farm® Herb Seasoned Stuffing

COOK sausage in medium skillet over medium-high heat until browned, stirring often. Pour off fat.

ADD water, onion and pepper. Heat to a boil. Cover and cook over low heat 5 minutes or until sausage is no longer pink.

ADD stuffing. Mix lightly. Cover and let stand 5 minutes.

Serves 4.

For moister stuffing, increase water to 1½ cups.

Chicken & Roasted Garlic Risotto

Prep/Cook Time: 20 minutes
Stand Time: 5 minutes

- 4   skinless, boneless chicken breast halves (about 1 pound)
- 1   tablespoon butter **or** margarine
- 1   can (10¾ ounces) Campbell's® Condensed Cream of Chicken **or** 98% Fat Free Cream of Chicken Soup
- 1   can (10¼ ounces) Campbell's® Condensed Cream of Mushroom with Roasted Garlic Soup
- 2   cups water
- 2   cups **uncooked** instant white rice
- 1   cup frozen peas and carrots

SEASON chicken.

HEAT butter in medium skillet over medium-high heat. Add chicken and cook 10 minutes or until browned. Set chicken aside.

ADD soups and water. Heat to a boil. Stir in rice and vegetables. Return chicken to skillet. Cover and cook over low heat 5 minutes or until chicken is no longer pink. Remove from heat. Let stand 5 minutes.

Serves 4.

Chicken & Roasted Garlic Risotto

Shortcut Stroganoff

Prep/Cook Time: 20 minutes

- 1 tablespoon vegetable oil
- 1 pound boneless beef sirloin steak strips
- 1 can (10¾ ounces) Campbell's® Condensed Cream of Mushroom **or** 98% Fat Free Cream of Mushroom Soup
- 1 can (10½ ounces) Campbell's® Condensed Beef Broth
- 1 cup water
- 2 teaspoons Worcestershire sauce
- 3 cups **uncooked** corkscrew pasta
- ½ cup sour cream

HEAT oil in medium skillet over medium-high heat. Add beef and cook until browned and juices evaporate, stirring often.

ADD soup, broth, water, Worcestershire and pasta. Heat to a boil. Cook over medium heat 15 minutes or until pasta is done, stirring often. Add sour cream. Heat through.

Serves 4.

Creamy Pesto Chicken & Bow Ties

Prep/Cook Time: 20 minutes

- 3 cups **uncooked** bow tie pasta
- 2 tablespoons butter **or** margarine
- 1 pound skinless, boneless chicken breasts, cut into cubes
- 1 can (10¾ ounces) Campbell's® Condensed Cream of Chicken **or** 98% Fat Free Cream of Chicken Soup
- ½ cup milk
- ½ cup prepared pesto sauce

COOK pasta according to package directions. Drain.

HEAT butter in medium skillet over medium-high heat. Add chicken and cook until browned, stirring often.

ADD soup, milk and pesto sauce. Heat to a boil. Cover and cook over low heat 5 minutes or until chicken is no longer pink. Stir in pasta and heat through.

Serves 4.

Creamy Pesto Chicken & Bow Ties

Pork with Roasted Peppers & Potatoes

Prep/Cook Time: 25 minutes

- 4 boneless pork chops, $\frac{1}{2}$-inch thick

  Ground black pepper

- 1 tablespoon olive oil
- 4 medium red potatoes, (about 1 pound), cut into 1-inch pieces
- 1 medium onion, sliced (about $\frac{1}{2}$ cup)
- 1 teaspoon dried oregano leaves, crushed
- 1 cup Swanson® Chicken **or** Natural Goodness™ Chicken Broth
- $\frac{1}{2}$ cup diced roasted sweet peppers

SEASON chops with black pepper.

HEAT oil in medium nonstick skillet over medium-high heat. Add chops and cook 10 minutes or until browned. Remove chops.

ADD potatoes, onion and oregano. Cook 5 minutes or until browned, stirring occasionally.

ADD broth and sweet peppers. Heat to a boil. Return chops to skillet. Cover and cook over low heat 10 minutes or until chops are no longer pink.

Serves 4.

Broccoli Chicken Potato Parmesan

Prep/Cook Time: 20 minutes

- 2 tablespoons vegetable oil
- 1 pound small red potatoes, sliced $\frac{1}{4}$-inch thick
- 1 package (about 10 ounces) refrigerated cooked chicken breast strips
- 2 cups fresh **or** frozen broccoli flowerets
- 1 can ($10\frac{3}{4}$ ounces) Campbell's® Condensed Broccoli Cheese **or** 98% Fat Free Broccoli Cheese Soup
- $\frac{1}{2}$ cup milk
- $\frac{1}{4}$ teaspoon garlic powder
- $\frac{1}{4}$ cup grated Parmesan cheese

HEAT oil in medium skillet over medium heat. Add potatoes. Cover and cook 10 minutes, stirring occasionally.

STIR in chicken and broccoli.

ADD soup, milk and garlic powder. Sprinkle with cheese. Heat to a boil. Cover and cook over low heat 5 minutes or until potatoes are tender.

Serves 4.

Broccoli Chicken Potato Parmesan

The
World's

Easy global cuisine with the accent on flavor

Fare

West African Vegetable Stew

Prep Time: 15 minutes
Cook Time: 30 minutes

1   tablespoon vegetable oil

2   cups sliced onions

2   cloves garlic, minced

2   sweet potatoes (about
    $1\frac{1}{2}$ pounds), peeled and
    cut in half lengthwise
    and sliced

1   large tomato, coarsely
    chopped ($1\frac{1}{2}$ cups)

1   can ($10\frac{1}{2}$ ounces)
    Campbell's® Condensed
    Chicken Broth

$\frac{1}{2}$ cup water

$\frac{1}{2}$ teaspoon **each** ground
    cinnamon **and** crushed
    red pepper

$\frac{1}{2}$ cup raisins

4   cups coarsely chopped
    fresh spinach leaves

1   can (about 15 ounces)
    chickpeas (garbanzo
    beans), rinsed and
    drained

    Hot cooked rice **or**
    couscous (optional)

HEAT oil in saucepot over
medium heat. Add onion and
garlic. Cook until onion is tender.

ADD potatoes and tomatoes.
Cook 5 minutes. Add broth, water,
cinnamon, red pepper and raisins.
Heat to a boil. Cover and cook
over low heat 15 minutes.

ADD spinach and chickpeas. Heat
through. Serve over rice or
couscous, if desired.

Serves 6.

Chicken Cacciatore & Pasta

Prep Time: 10 minutes
Cook Time: 30 minutes

1   tablespoon vegetable oil

4   skinless, boneless chicken breast halves **or** 8 boneless chicken thighs, skin removed (about 1 pound)

1   can (14 ounces) Swanson® Chicken **or** Natural Goodness™ Chicken Broth (1¾ cups)

1   teaspoon dried oregano leaves, crushed

½   teaspoon garlic powder

1   can (14 ounces) whole peeled tomatoes, cut up

1   small green pepper, cut into 2-inch-long strips (about 1 cup)

1   medium onion, cut into wedges

2½   cups **uncooked** medium shell pasta

HEAT oil in medium skillet over medium-high heat. Add chicken and cook 10 minutes or until browned.

ADD broth, oregano, garlic powder, tomatoes, pepper and onion. Heat to a boil. Stir in pasta. Cover and cook over low heat 15 minutes or until pasta is done.

Serves 4.

Creamy Enchiladas Verde

Prep Time: 10 minutes
Bake Time: 20 minutes

1   can (10¾ ounces) Campbell's® Condensed Creamy Chicken Verde Soup

½   teaspoon garlic powder

1½   cups chopped cooked chicken

⅔   cup shredded Cheddar **or** Monterey Jack cheese (about 4 ounces)

8   corn tortillas (6-inch), warmed

¼   cup milk

MIX ½ can soup, garlic powder, chicken and ⅓ **cup** cheese.

SPOON about ⅓ cup chicken mixture down center of each tortilla. Roll tortilla around filling and place seam-side down in 2-quart shallow baking dish. Mix remaining soup and milk and pour over all. Top with remaining cheese.

BAKE at 375°F. for 20 minutes or until hot.

Serves 4.

Creamy Enchiladas Verde

Mediterranean Chicken & Rice Bake

Prep Time: 10 minutes
Bake Time: 50 minutes

1   can (14 ounces) Swanson®
    Chicken **or** Natural
    Goodness™ Chicken
    Broth (1¾ cups)

¼   cup chopped fresh parsley

¼   cup sliced pitted ripe olives

1   tablespoon fresh lemon
    juice

¼   teaspoon ground black
    pepper

1   can (about 14½ ounces)
    stewed tomatoes

1¼ cups **uncooked** regular
    long-grain white rice

6   skinless, boneless chicken
    breast halves (about
    1½ pounds)

½   teaspoon garlic powder

    Paprika

MIX broth, parsley, olives, lemon
juice, black pepper, tomatoes and
rice in 3-quart shallow baking dish.
Cover.

BAKE at 375°F. for 20 minutes.

PLACE chicken on rice mixture.
Sprinkle with garlic powder and
paprika.

BAKE for 30 minutes or until
chicken is no longer pink and rice is
done.

Serves 6.

Zesty Rice with Chorizo

Prep Time: 10 minutes
Cook Time: 30 minutes

1   tablespoon vegetable oil

1   package (3½ ounces)
    chorizo sausage, cut into
    cubes

1   medium onion, chopped
    (about ½ cup)

2   cloves garlic, minced

1   can (14 ounces) Swanson®
    Chicken **or** Natural
    Goodness™ Chicken
    Broth (1¾ cups)

½   cup Pace® Chunky Salsa*

¾   cup **uncooked** regular
    long-grain white rice

½   cup frozen peas

    Chopped fresh cilantro
    leaves

HEAT oil in medium skillet over
medium-high heat. Add sausage,
onion and garlic and cook until
onion is tender.

ADD broth, salsa and rice. Heat to a
boil. Cover and cook over low heat
15 minutes. Stir in peas. Cover and
cook 5 minutes or until rice is
done. Sprinkle with cilantro.

Serves 4.

**Also delicious with Pace® Chipotle
Chunky Salsa.*

Zesty Rice with Chorizo

Moroccan Lamb Stew

Prep Time: 15 minutes
Cook Time: 1 hour 35 minutes

1   tablespoon olive oil

2   pounds lamb for stew, cut into 1-inch pieces

$\frac{1}{2}$ teaspoon ground cinnamon

$\frac{1}{4}$ teaspoon ground cloves

1   medium onion, chopped (about $\frac{1}{2}$ cup)

1   box (32 ounces) Swanson® Chicken **or** Natural Goodness™ Chicken Broth (4 cups)

1   cup dried lentils

2   medium potatoes, cut into cubes (about 2 cups)

Hot cooked couscous (optional)

Chopped fresh cilantro leaves (optional)

HEAT oil in large saucepot over medium-high heat. Add **half** of lamb and cook until browned, stirring often. Remove lamb. Repeat. Sprinkle cinnamon and cloves over lamb and stir until coated.

ADD onion and cook over medium heat until tender-crisp. Return lamb to saucepot. Add broth. Heat to a boil. Cover and cook over low heat 1 hour.

ADD lentils and potatoes. Cook 20 minutes or until lentils and potatoes are tender. Serve over couscous and sprinkle with cilantro, if desired.

Serves 8.

Italian-Style Pot Roast

Prep Time: 5 minutes
Cook Time: 3 hours

2   tablespoons vegetable oil

$3\frac{1}{2}$- to 4-pound boneless beef bottom round **or** chuck pot roast

1   jar (1 pound 10 ounces) Prego® Traditional Pasta Sauce

6   medium potatoes (about $1\frac{1}{2}$ pounds), cut into quarters

6   medium carrots (about $\frac{3}{4}$ pound), cut into 2-inch pieces

HEAT oil in saucepot. Add roast and cook until browned on all sides. Pour off fat.

ADD pasta sauce. Heat to a boil. Cover and cook over low heat 1 hour 45 minutes.

ADD potatoes and carrots. Cover and cook over low heat 1 hour or until roast and vegetables are tender.

Serves 8.

Moroccan Lamb Stew

Mexican Lasagna

Prep Time: 30 minutes
Bake Time: 20 minutes
Stand Time: 5 minutes

1 pound ground beef

1 large green pepper, chopped (about 1 cup)

2 cups Prego® Traditional Pasta Sauce

1½ cups Pace® Picante Sauce

1 tablespoon chili powder

8 flour tortillas (6-inch)

2 cups shredded Cheddar cheese (8 ounces)

2 cans (2¼ ounces **each**) sliced pitted ripe olives, drained

COOK beef and pepper in medium skillet over medium-high heat until beef is browned, stirring to separate meat. Pour off fat.

ADD pasta sauce, **1 cup** picante sauce and chili powder. Heat to a boil. Cook over low heat 10 minutes.

SPREAD remaining picante sauce in 3-quart shallow baking dish. Arrange **4** tortillas in dish. Top with **half** the beef mixture, **half** the cheese and **half** the olives. Repeat layers.

BAKE at 350°F. for 20 minutes or until hot. Let stand 5 minutes.

Serves 8.

TIP:
Substitute **1 pound** skinless, boneless chicken halves, cut into cubes, for the ground beef.

Spicy Salsa Mac & Beef

Prep/Cook Time: 20 minutes

1 pound ground beef

1 can (10½ ounces) Campbell's® Condensed Beef Broth

1⅓ cups water

2 cups **uncooked** medium shell pasta

1 can (10¾ ounces) Campbell's® Condensed Cheddar Cheese Soup

1 cup Pace® Chunky Salsa

COOK beef in medium skillet over medium-high heat until browned, stirring to separate meat. Pour off fat.

ADD broth and water. Heat to a boil. Add pasta. Cook over medium heat 10 minutes or until pasta is done, stirring often.

ADD soup and salsa. Heat through.

Serves 4.

Spicy Salsa Mac & Beef

Asian Chicken & Rice Bake

Prep Time: 5 minutes
Bake Time: 45 minutes

$\frac{3}{4}$ cup **uncooked** regular long-grain white rice

4 skinless, boneless chicken breast halves (about 1 pound)

1 can (10$\frac{3}{4}$ ounces) Campbell's® Condensed Golden Mushroom Soup

$\frac{3}{4}$ cup water

2 tablespoons soy sauce

2 tablespoons cider vinegar

2 tablespoons honey

1 teaspoon garlic powder

Paprika

SPREAD rice in 2-quart shallow baking dish. Top with chicken.

MIX soup, water, soy, vinegar, honey and garlic powder. Pour over chicken. Sprinkle with paprika. **Cover.**

BAKE at 375°F. for 45 minutes or until chicken is no longer pink.

Serves 4.

Steak & Mushroom Florentine

Prep Time: 10 minutes
Cook Time: 10 minutes

1 pound boneless beef sirloin **or** top round steak, $\frac{3}{4}$-inch thick

2 tablespoons vegetable oil

1 small onion, sliced (about $\frac{1}{4}$ cup)

4 cups baby spinach leaves, washed

1 can (10$\frac{3}{4}$ ounces) Campbell's® Condensed Cream of Mushroom **or** 98% Fat Free Cream of Mushroom Soup

1 cup water

1 large tomato, thickly sliced

Freshly ground black pepper

SLICE beef into very thin strips.

HEAT 1 tablespoon oil in medium nonstick skillet over medium-high heat. Add beef and cook until browned and juices evaporate, stirring often. Set beef aside.

HEAT remaining oil over medium heat. Add onion and cook until tender-crisp. Add spinach and cook just until spinach is wilted.

ADD soup and water. Heat to a boil. Return beef to skillet and heat through. Serve beef mixture over tomato. Season to taste with black pepper.

Serves 4.

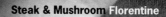
Steak & Mushroom Florentine

Jollof Chicken & Rice

Prep Time: 15 minutes
Cook Time: 40 minutes
Stand Time: 5 minutes

1 tablespoon vegetable oil

2½- to 3½-pound broiler-fryer chicken, cut up

1 cup chopped onion

2 cloves garlic, minced

4 plum tomatoes, coarsely chopped (about 2 cups)

1 can (10½ ounces) Campbell's® Condensed Chicken Broth

½ cup water

½ teaspoon crushed red pepper

Few saffron threads **or** ¼ teaspoon ground turmeric

1 cup **uncooked** regular long-grain white rice

1 cup coarsely chopped fresh spinach leaves

HEAT oil in large skillet over medium-high heat. Add chicken and cook 10 minutes or until browned. Remove chicken.

ADD onion and garlic and cook over medium heat until tender. Add tomatoes and cook 2 minutes. Add broth, water, red pepper, saffron and rice. Heat to a boil. Return chicken to skillet. Cover and cook over low heat 25 minutes or until chicken is no longer pink.

STIR in spinach. Let stand 5 minutes.

Serves 4.

Surefire shortcuts to favorite family standards

Quick & Easy
Classics

Quick Chicken Parmesan

Prep/Bake Time: 15 minutes

2   cups Prego® Traditional Pasta Sauce

4   fully cooked breaded chicken cutlets

4   thin slices cooked ham

1   cup shredded mozzarella cheese (4 ounces)

2   tablespoons grated Parmesan cheese

SPREAD 1 cup pasta sauce in 2-quart shallow baking dish.

ARRANGE chicken over sauce. Spoon ¼ **cup** sauce down center of each cutlet. Top each with **1 slice** ham and ¼ **cup** mozzarella cheese. Sprinkle with Parmesan cheese.

BAKE at 425°F. for 10 minutes or until cheese is melted and sauce bubbles.

Serves 4.

Quick Chicken Parmesan

Chicken and Biscuits Casserole

Prep Time: 10 minutes
Bake Time: 30 minutes

1   can (10¾ ounces) Campbell's® Condensed Cream of Celery **or** 98% Fat Free Cream of Celery Soup

1   can (10¾ ounces) Campbell's® Condensed Cream of Potato Soup

1   cup milk

¼   teaspoon dried thyme leaves, crushed

¼   teaspoon ground black pepper

4   cups cooked cut-up vegetables*

2   cups cubed cooked chicken

1   package (about 7 ounces) refrigerated buttermilk biscuits (10)

MIX soups, milk, thyme, black pepper, vegetables and chicken in 3-quart shallow baking dish.

BAKE at 400°F. for 15 minutes. Stir. Cut each biscuit into quarters.

ARRANGE cut biscuits over chicken mixture. Bake for 15 minutes or until biscuits are golden.

Serves 5.

*Use a combination of broccoli flowerets, cauliflower flowerets and carrots.

Miracle Lasagna

Prep Time: 5 minutes
Bake Time: 1 hour
Stand Time: 5 minutes

1 jar (1 pound 10 ounces) Prego® Traditional Pasta Sauce

6 **uncooked** lasagna noodles

1 container (15 ounces) ricotta cheese

2 cups shredded mozzarella cheese (8 ounces)

¼ cup grated Parmesan cheese

SPREAD about **1 cup** pasta sauce in 2-quart shallow baking dish (11×7-inch). Top with **3 uncooked** noodles, ricotta cheese, **1 cup** mozzarella cheese, Parmesan cheese and **1 cup** pasta sauce. Top with remaining **3 uncooked** noodles and remaining pasta sauce. **Cover.**

BAKE at 375°F. for 1 hour. Uncover and top with remaining mozzarella cheese. Let stand 5 minutes.

Serves 6.

Easy Chicken Pot Pie

Prep Time: 10 minutes
Bake Time: 30 minutes

1 can (10¾ ounces) Campbell's® Condensed Cream of Chicken **or** 98% Fat Free Cream of Chicken Soup*

1 package (about 9 ounces) frozen mixed vegetables, thawed

1 cup cubed cooked chicken **or** turkey

½ cup milk

1 egg

1 cup all-purpose baking mix

PREHEAT oven to 400°F.

MIX soup, vegetables and chicken in 9-inch pie plate.

MIX milk, egg and baking mix. Pour over chicken mixture.

BAKE for 30 minutes or until golden.

Serves 4.

Substitute Campbell's® Condensed Cream of Chicken with Herbs Soup for the Cream of Chicken Soup.

Easy Chicken Pot Pie

Southern Cornbread Turkey Pot Pie

Prep/Bake Time: 25 minutes

1   can (10¾ ounces) Campbell's® Condensed Cream of Chicken **or** 98% Fat Free Cream of Chicken Soup

⅛   teaspoon ground black pepper

2   cups cubed cooked turkey **or** chicken

1   can (about 8 ounces) whole kernel corn, drained

1   package (11 ounces) refrigerated cornbread twists

PREHEAT oven to 425°F.

MIX soup, black pepper, turkey and corn in medium saucepan over medium heat. Heat through. Pour turkey mixture into 9-inch pie plate.

SEPARATE cornbread into **8** pieces along perforations. (Do not unroll dough.) Place over hot turkey mixture. Bake for 15 minutes or until bread is golden.

Serves 4.

Pork & Corn Stuffing Bake

Prep Time: 10 minutes
Bake Time: 30 minutes

1½   cups Pepperidge Farm® Cornbread Stuffing **or** Herb Seasoned Stuffing

1   can (10¾ ounces) Campbell's® Condensed Cream of Celery **or** 98% Fat Free Cream of Celery Soup

½   cup whole kernel corn

1   small onion, finely chopped (about ¼ cup)

¼   cup finely chopped celery

4   boneless pork chops, ¾-inch thick (about 1 pound)

1   tablespoon packed brown sugar

1   teaspoon spicy-brown mustard

MIX stuffing, soup, corn, onion and celery. Spoon into greased 9-inch pie plate. Top with chops.

MIX brown sugar and mustard and spoon over chops.

BAKE at 400°F. for 30 minutes or until chops are no longer pink.

Serves 4.

Pork & Corn Stuffing Bake

Savory Pot Roast & Harvest Vegetables

Prep Time: 15 minutes
Cook Time: 2 hours 30 minutes

2   tablespoons vegetable oil

    3-pound boneless beef
    bottom round **or** chuck
    pot roast

1   can (14 ounces)
    Swanson® Seasoned
    Beef Broth with Onion

¾   cup V8® 100% Vegetable
    Juice

3   medium potatoes
    (about ¼ pound), cut
    into quarters

3   stalks celery, cut into
    1-inch pieces (about
    2¼ cups)

2   cups fresh **or** frozen baby
    carrots

2   tablespoons all-purpose
    flour

¼   cup water

HEAT oil in saucepot over medium-high heat. Add roast and cook until browned on all sides. Pour off fat.

ADD broth and vegetable juice. Heat to a boil. Cover and cook over low heat 1 hour 45 minutes.

ADD potatoes, celery and carrots. Cover and cook 30 minutes or until vegetables are tender. Remove roast and vegetables and keep warm.

MIX flour and water. Add to saucepot. Cook over medium heat until mixture boils and thickens, stirring constantly. Serve with roast and vegetables.

Serves 6.

Easy Beef Pot Pie

Prep Time: 20 minutes
Bake Time: 40 minutes

$\frac{1}{2}$ package (15 ounces)
    refrigerated pie crusts
    (1 crust)

2 cups diced cooked potatoes

1 package (10 ounces) frozen
    mixed vegetables, thawed
    (about 10 cups)

$1\frac{1}{2}$ cups diced cooked beef

1 can ($10\frac{3}{4}$ ounces)
    Campbell's® Condensed
    Golden Mushroom Soup

$\frac{1}{3}$ cup water

1 teaspoon Worcestershire
    sauce

1 teaspoon dried thyme
    leaves, crushed

PREHEAT oven to 400°F. Bring
pie crust to room temperature.

ARRANGE potatoes, vegetables
and beef in 9-inch deep-dish pie
plate **or** $1\frac{1}{2}$-quart casserole. Mix
soup, water, Worcestershire and
thyme. Pour over beef mixture.

PLACE pie crust over beef
mixture. Flute edges. Cut slits in
crust.

BAKE for 35 minutes or until hot
and crust is browned.

Serves 4.

Sausage-Stuffed Green Peppers

Prep Time: 20 minutes
Bake Time: 40 minutes

1 tablespoon vegetable oil

1 pound sweet Italian pork
    sausage, casing removed

1 medium onion, chopped
    (about $\frac{1}{2}$ cup)

1 teaspoon dried oregano
    leaves, crushed

1 cup shredded part-skim
    mozzarella cheese
    (4 ounces)

4 medium green peppers,
    seeded and cut in half
    lengthwise

2 cups Prego® Traditional
    Pasta Sauce

HEAT oil in medium skillet over
medium-high heat. Cook sausage
until browned, stirring to separate
meat. Add onion and oregano and
cook until tender. Pour off fat. Stir
in cheese.

ARRANGE peppers in 3-quart
shallow baking dish **or** roasting
pan. Spoon sausage mixture into
peppers. Pour pasta sauce over
peppers. **Cover.**

BAKE at 400°F. for 40 minutes or
until peppers are tender.

Serves 8.

Sausage-Stuffed Green Peppers

Tuna & Pasta Cheddar Melt

Prep/Cook Time: 20 minutes

1 can ($10\frac{1}{2}$ ounces)
   Campbell's® Condensed
   Chicken Broth

1 soup can water

3 cups **uncooked** corkscrew
   pasta

1 can ($10\frac{3}{4}$ ounces)
   Campbell's® Condensed
   Cream of Mushroom **or**
   98% Fat Free Cream of
   Mushroom Soup

1 cup milk

1 can (about 6 ounces) tuna,
   drained and flaked

1 cup shredded Cheddar
   cheese (4 ounces)

2 tablespoons Italian-
   seasoned dry bread
   crumbs

2 teaspoons butter **or**
   margarine, melted

HEAT broth and water to a boil over high heat in medium skillet. Add pasta and cook until just tender, stirring often. Do not drain.

ADD soup, milk and tuna. Top with cheese. Mix bread crumbs with butter and sprinkle on top. Heat through.

Serves 4.

Chicken Broccoli Divan

Prep Time: 15 minutes
Bake Time: 25 minutes

1   pound fresh broccoli, cut
    into spears **or** 1 package
    (about 10 ounces)
    frozen broccoli spears,
    cooked and drained

$1\frac{1}{2}$ cups cubed cooked
    chicken **or** turkey

1   can ($10\frac{3}{4}$ ounces)
    Campbell's® Condensed
    Broccoli Cheese **or**
    98% Fat Free Broccoli
    Cheese Soup*

$\frac{1}{3}$ cup milk

$\frac{1}{2}$ cup shredded Cheddar
    cheese (optional)

2   tablespoons dry bread
    crumbs

1   tablespoon butter **or**
    margarine, melted

ARRANGE broccoli and chicken
in 9-inch pie plate or 2-quart
shallow baking dish.

MIX soup and milk and pour
over broccoli and chicken.

SPRINKLE with cheese. Mix
bread crumbs with butter and
sprinkle on top.

BAKE at 400°F. for 25 minutes or
until hot.

Serves 4.

*Substitute 1 can ($10\frac{3}{4}$ ounces)
Campbell's® Condensed Cream of
Chicken **or** 98% Fat Free Cream of
Chicken Soup for the Broccoli
Cheese Soup.*

TIP:
For **1$\frac{1}{2}$ cups** cubed cooked
chicken, cook $\frac{3}{4}$ **pound** skinless,
boneless chicken breasts, cut into
cubes, in medium saucepan over
medium heat, in **4 cups** boiling
water for 5 minutes or until
chicken is no longer pink.

Super Bowl Chili Beans & Rice

Prep Time: 10 minutes
Cook Time: 25 minutes

Vegetable cooking spray

$1\frac{1}{2}$ pounds skinless, boneless chicken breasts, cut into cubes

1 can (14 ounces) Swanson® Chicken **or** Natural Goodness™ Chicken Broth ($1\frac{3}{4}$ cups)

2 tablespoons chili powder

2 medium tomatoes, chopped (about 2 cups)

1 medium green pepper, chopped (about $\frac{3}{4}$ cup)

1 cup **uncooked** regular long-grain white rice

2 cans (16 ounces **each**) Campbell's® Pork & Beans

$\frac{1}{2}$ cup fat-free sour cream

Sliced green onions (optional)

SPRAY saucepot with cooking spray and heat over medium-high heat 1 minute. Add chicken and cook until browned, stirring often.

ADD broth, chili powder, tomatoes, pepper, rice and beans. Heat to a boil. Cover and cook over low heat 20 minutes or until rice is done. Top with sour cream and green onions, if desired.

Serves 8.

25-Minute Chicken & Noodles

Prep/Cook Time: 25 minutes

1 can (14 ounces) Swanson® Chicken **or** Natural Goodness™ Chicken Broth ($1\frac{1}{4}$ cups)

$\frac{1}{2}$ teaspoon dried basil leaves, crushed

$\frac{1}{8}$ teaspoon ground black pepper

2 cups frozen vegetable combination (broccoli, cauliflower, carrots)

2 cups **uncooked** medium egg noodles

2 cups cubed cooked chicken

MIX broth, basil, black pepper and vegetables in medium skillet over high heat. Heat to a boil. Cover and cook over low heat 5 minutes.

STIR in noodles. Cover and cook 5 minutes. Add chicken and heat through.

Serves 4.

25-Minute Chicken & Noodles

Green Bean Casserole

Prep Time: 10 minutes
Bake Time: 30 minutes

1   can (10¾ ounces)
    Campbell's® Condensed
    Cream of Mushroom **or**
    98% Fat Free Cream of
    Mushroom Soup

½   cup milk

1   teaspoon soy sauce
    Dash ground black pepper

4   cups cooked cut green
    beans

1⅓ cups French's® French
    Fried Onions

MIX soup, milk, soy, black
pepper, beans and ⅔ **cup** onions
in 1½-quart casserole.

BAKE at 350°F. for 25 minutes or
until hot.

STIR. Sprinkle with remaining
onions. Bake 5 minutes.

Serves 6.

TIP:
Use **1 bag** (16 to 20 ounces)
frozen green beans, **2 packages**
(9 ounces **each**) frozen green
beans, **2 cans** (about 16 ounces
each) green beans **or** about
1½-**pounds** fresh green beans for
this recipe.

Shortcut Beef Stew

Prep/Cook Time: 20 minutes

1 tablespoon vegetable oil

1 pound boneless beef
   sirloin, cut into 1-inch
   pieces

1 can (10¾ ounces)
   Campbell's® Condensed
   Tomato Soup

1 can (10½ ounces)
   Campbell's® Condensed
   French Onion Soup

1 tablespoon Worcestershire
   sauce

1 bag (24 ounces) frozen
   vegetables for stew
   (potatoes, carrots,
   celery)*

HEAT oil in skillet over medium-high heat. Add beef and cook until browned and juices evaporate, stirring often.

ADD soups, Worcestershire and vegetables. Heat to a boil. Cover and cook over low heat 10 minutes or until vegetables are tender.

Serves 4.

*Substitute **5 cups** frozen vegetables (carrots, small whole onions, cut green beans, cauliflower, zucchini, peas or lima beans) for the frozen vegetables for stew.*

Casseroles and One-Dish Meals 97

METRIC CONVERSION CHART

VOLUME MEASUREMENTS (dry)

⅛ teaspoon = 0.5 mL
¼ teaspoon = 1 mL
½ teaspoon = 2 mL
¾ teaspoon = 4 mL
1 teaspoon = 5 mL
1 tablespoon = 15 mL
2 tablespoons = 30 mL
¼ cup = 60 mL
⅓ cup = 75 mL
½ cup = 125 mL
⅔ cup = 150 mL
¾ cup = 175 mL
1 cup = 250 mL
2 cups = 1 pint = 500 mL
3 cups = 750 mL
4 cups = 1 quart = 1 L

VOLUME MEASUREMENTS (fluid)

1 fluid ounce (2 tablespoons) = 30 mL
4 fluid ounces (½ cup) = 125 mL
8 fluid ounces (1 cup) = 250 mL
12 fluid ounces (1½ cups) = 375 mL
16 fluid ounces (2 cups) = 500 mL

WEIGHTS (mass)

½ ounce = 15 g
1 ounce = 30 g
3 ounces = 90 g
4 ounces = 120 g
8 ounces = 225 g
10 ounces = 285 g
12 ounces = 360 g
16 ounces = 1 pound = 450 g

DIMENSIONS

1/16 inch = 2 mm
⅛ inch = 3 mm
¼ inch = 6 mm
½ inch = 1.5 cm
¾ inch = 2 cm
1 inch = 2.5 cm

OVEN TEMPERATURES

250°F = 120°C
275°F = 140°C
300°F = 150°C
325°F = 160°C
350°F = 180°C
375°F = 190°C
400°F = 200°C
425°F = 220°C
450°F = 230°C

BAKING PAN SIZES

Utensil	Size in Inches/Quarts	Metric Volume	Size in Centimeters
Baking or	82 82 2	2 L	202 202 5
Cake Pan	92 92 2	2.5 L	232 232 5
(square or	122 82 2	3 L	302 202 5
rectangular)	132 92 2	3.5 L	332 232 5
Loaf Pan	82 42 3	1.5 L	202 102 7
	92 52 3	2 L	232 132 7
Round Layer	82 1½	1.2 L	202 4
Cake Pan	92 1½	1.5 L	232 4
Pie Plate	82 1¼	750 mL	202 3
	92 1¼	1 L	232 3
Baking Dish	1 quart	1 L	—
or Casserole	1½ quart	1.5 L	—
	2 quart	2 L	—

Simple Winter